INSIDE PROFESSIONAL SOCCER

SL BENFICA

Heather DiLorenzo Williams

MEDIA ENHANCED BOOKS
AV² BY WEIGL
ADDED VALUE • AUDIO VISUAL
www.av2books.com

Go to **www.av2books.com,** and enter this book's unique code.

BOOK CODE

AVJ28596

AV² by Weigl brings you media enhanced books that support active learning.

AV² provides enriched content that supplements and complements this book. Weigl's AV² books strive to create inspired learning and engage young minds in a total learning experience.

Your AV² Media Enhanced books come alive with...

Audio
Listen to sections of the book read aloud.

Key Words
Study vocabulary, and complete a matching word activity.

Video
Watch informative video clips.

Quizzes
Test your knowledge.

Embedded Weblinks
Gain additional information for research.

Slide Show
View images and captions, and prepare a presentation.

Try This!
Complete activities and hands-on experiments.

... and much, much more!

Published by AV² by Weigl
350 5th Avenue, 59th Floor
New York, NY 10118
Website: www.av2books.com

Library of Congress Control Number: 2018968476

ISBN 978-1-7911-0598-3 (hardcover)
ISBN 978-1-7911-0599-0 (multi-user eBook)
ISBN 978-1-7911-0600-3 (single-user eBook)

Printed in Guangzhou, China
1 2 3 4 5 6 7 8 9 0 23 22 21 20 19

022019
102318

Project Coordinator: John Willis Designer: Terry Paulhus

Every reasonable effort has been made to trace ownership and to obtain permission to reprint copyright material. The publishers would be pleased to have any errors or omissions brought to their attention so that they may be corrected in subsequent printings.

The publisher acknowledges Alamy, Getty Images, iStock, and Wikimedia as its primary image suppliers for this title.

CONTENTS

AV2 Book Code 2
Introduction 4
History 6
The Arena 8
Where They Play 10
The Uniforms 12
Goalie Gear 14
The Coaches 16
Fans Around the World 18
Legends of the Past 20
Stars of Today 22
All-Time Records 24
Timeline 26
Write a Biography 28
Trivia Time 30
Key Words/Index 31
www.av2books.com 32

Introduction

Lisbon, Portugal, is one of the world's oldest cities. It is surrounded by seven distinct hills and sits next to the Atlantic Ocean. Visitors to Lisbon can lounge on the beach or visit one of many centuries-old castles. They can also take in a soccer match. Lisbon is home to one of Europe's best-known soccer **clubs**.

Sport Lisboa e Benfica is also known as SL Benfica, or just Benfica. It is a sports club that includes soccer, basketball, cycling, and rugby. Soccer is the most popular. The club is the biggest and most supported in Portugal.

Benfica is one of 18 teams in the *Primeira Liga*, or "Premier League," Portugal's top division of soccer. Benfica is considered one of the "Big Three" Portuguese teams, along with rivals Sporting CP and FC Porto. Many consider Benfica to be the most **decorated** club in Europe.

Benfica's Franco Cervi scored a goal in his debut game with the team in 2016.

Andrija Živković signed a five-year contract with Benfica after playing three seasons with a club in his home country of Serbia.

SL BENFICA

Arena Estádio da Luz

Division Primeira Liga

Head Coach Rui Vitória

Location Lisbon, Portugal

FIFA Club World Cups 0

Nicknames *Águias* ("Eagles"), *Encarnados* ("Reds"), *O Glorioso* ("Glorious One")

6 Home Fields

26 Portuguese Cups

2 European Champion Clubs' Cups

38 Champions' League Appearances

78 Major Trophies

History

Benfica captain José Águas led his team to a 5–3 win against Real Madrid to claim the 1962 European Cup.

SL Benfica was founded in 1904 as Sport Lisboa by a group of young men led by Cosme Damião. In 1908, Sport Lisboa merged with Grupo Sport Benfica and became Sport Lisboa e Benfica. In its early days, the club did not have much money and had to play on a dirt field. Some players became frustrated and moved to another club, the newly formed Sporting CP. A fierce rivalry grew between the two teams. They remain rivals to this day.

The Primeira Liga was established in 1934. Benfica won the division title in 1936, 1937, and 1938, and would go on to dominate the league for decades. Benfica was the first Portuguese team to win the European Cup, which they were awarded two years in a row in 1961 and 1962. Although Benfica was one of Europe's dominant teams in the decades that followed, they never won another European title.

Benfica was successful in Portugal throughout the '80s and '90s. However, financial issues and coaching conflicts plagued the team until 2003. A new owner, a new coach, and a new stadium brought about a new era in the mid-2000s. Benfica won the Primeira Liga title in 2005 for the first time in more than a decade, restoring the team's reputation as Portugal's dominant club.

Luís Filipe Vieira is SL Benfica's 33rd president. He was elected in 2003.

The Arena

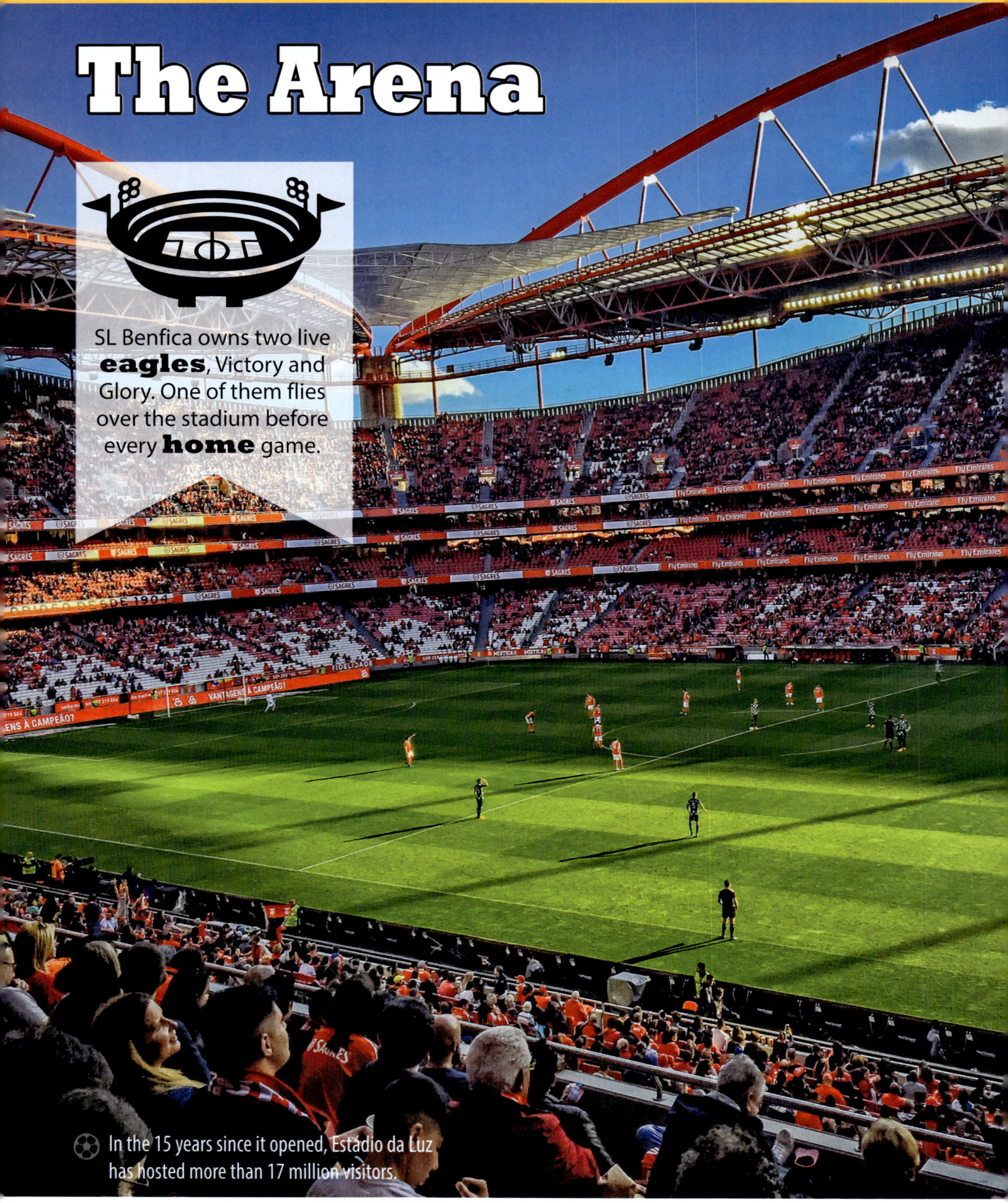

SL Benfica owns two live **eagles**, Victory and Glory. One of them flies over the stadium before every **home** game.

In the 15 years since it opened, Estádio da Luz has hosted more than 17 million visitors.

In its early days, SL Benfica played at several rented fields. In 1925, Estádio das Amoreiras became the team's home grounds. After 15 years, the team moved to Estádio do Campo Grande. Estádio da Luz opened in 1954, and the site has been Benfica's home ever since.

The original Estádio da Luz was demolished in 2002. The current stadium was rebuilt in its exact location. Today, Estádio da Luz is the largest stadium in Portugal. The stadium seats around 65,000 people. Every seat provides an unobstructed view of the field. It is named for the Church of Our Lady of the Light. *Estádio da Luz* translates to "stadium of light," but the name also refers to its location in the Luz neighborhood of Lisbon.

Estádio da Luz is home to the *Museu Benfica Cosme Damião*, the "Cosme Damião Benfica Museum." This museum is dedicated to the club's history and contains every trophy the club has won in all sports. A golden eagle with the club's motto, *E pluribus unum*, hangs over the stadium's main entrance. The motto is Latin for "Out of many, one." A statue of the club's legendary **forward** Eusébio stands outside the stadium.

Visitors to Museu Benfica Cosme Damião are greeted by a life-size hologram of Eusébio and video walls displaying photos of Benfica fans.

Where They Play

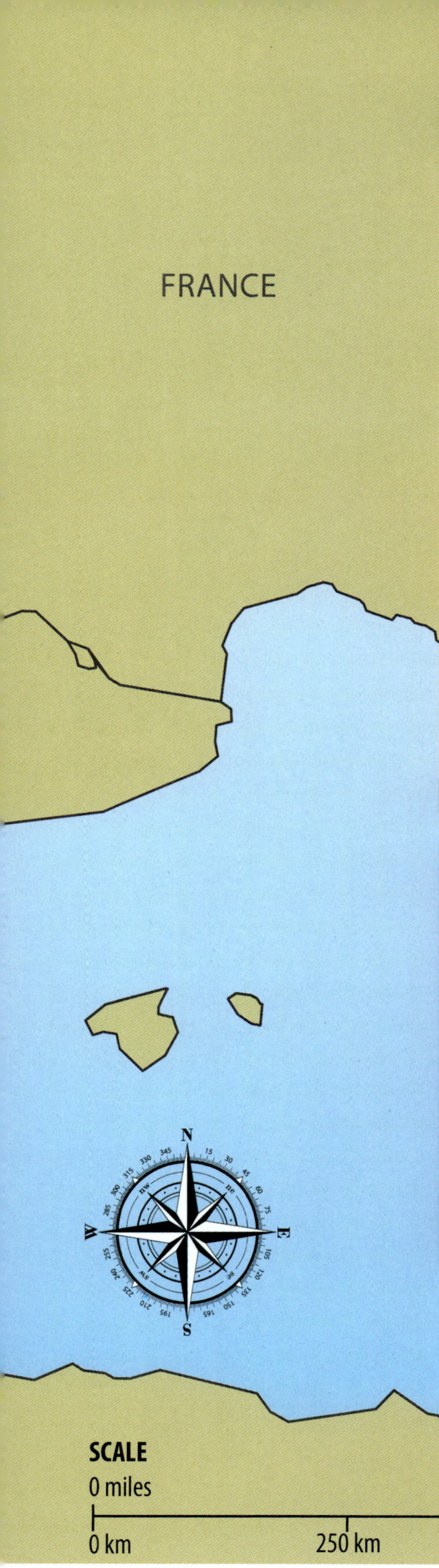

Arena
Estádio da Luz

Location
Lisbon, Portugal

Broke Ground
2002

Completed
October 25, 2003

Field Design
A standard natural grass pitch is surrounded by four red steel arches that support a polycarbonate roof. This allows the stadium to be illuminated by natural light, and also to appear as if it is glowing.

Features
- Names of sponsors, such as Coca-Cola, and images of cheering fans formed by red and white seats.
- Voted Europe's most beautiful stadium in 2014.
- Referred to as "the Cathedral" by fans.

2018–19 PRIMEIRA LIGA TEAMS

1 Belenenses *(Lisbon)*
★ 2 Benfica *(Lisbon)*
3 Boavista *(Porto)*
4 Braga *(Braga)*
5 Chaves *(Chaves)*
6 Desportivo das Aves *(Aves)*
7 Feirense *(Santa Maria da Feira)*
8 Marítimo *(Funchal)*
9 Moreirense *(Moreira de Cónegos)*
10 Nacional *(Funchal)*
11 Portimonense *(Portimão)*
12 Porto *(Porto)*
13 Rio Ave *(Vila do Conde)*
14 Santa Clara *(Ponta Delgada)*
15 Sporting CP *(Lisbon)*
16 Tondela *(Tondela)*
17 Vitória de Guimarães *(Guimarães)*
18 Vitória de Setúbal *(Setúbal)*

The Uniforms

Benfica's traditional red shirts feature three stars above the club's crest. Each star represents 10 Primeira Liga title wins.

SL Benfica's founders decided on the club's colors early in the club's history. These colors have changed very little in more than a century. Players have always worn red to symbolize bravery and white to symbolize peace. Benfica's home **kit** includes a red shirt and red, black, or white shorts and socks. The away kit is typically black, black and gold, or black and white.

Benfica's logo combines an eagle emblem, for Sport Lisboa, and a bike wheel, for Sport Benfica, to represent the two clubs that merged to form SL Benfica. A red and white crest with the club's initials and a golden ball are at the center. There is a red and green banner at the top with the club's motto. Much like the club's colors, the logo has not changed much in more than 100 years.

The golden eagle is an important symbol for Benfica. It represents independence, nobility, and authority.

Goalie Gear

Goalkeeper Odysseas Vlachodimos was promoted to starting goalie just a few months after he signed with the club. The young keeper, known simply as Odysseas, impressed Benfica's head coach in pre-season games and training sessions.

A team's **goalkeeper** must stand out from the other players on the field. Goalies usually wear long sleeves and brightly colored jerseys. The current Benfica goalkeeper jersey is either white or bright yellow. Goalkeepers can wear pants instead of shorts if they choose. Most goalies wear special gloves that contain plastic spines. These spines protect goalies' hands from injuries. Goalie gloves usually have rubbery surfaces to help the goalie grip the ball.

One of Benfica's most legendary goalkeepers was Michel Preud'homme. Preud'homme was known for making impossible saves and was nicknamed "Saint Michel." Benfica's current goalkeepers are Mile Svilar, Bruno Varela, and Odysseas Vlachodimos. Svilar and Varela signed with Benfica in 2017, while Vlachodimos joined the team for the 2018–19 season. Benfica's goalkeepers are all considered to be young players. At age 18, Mile Svilar holds the record for being the youngest goalkeeper to play in the Champions League.

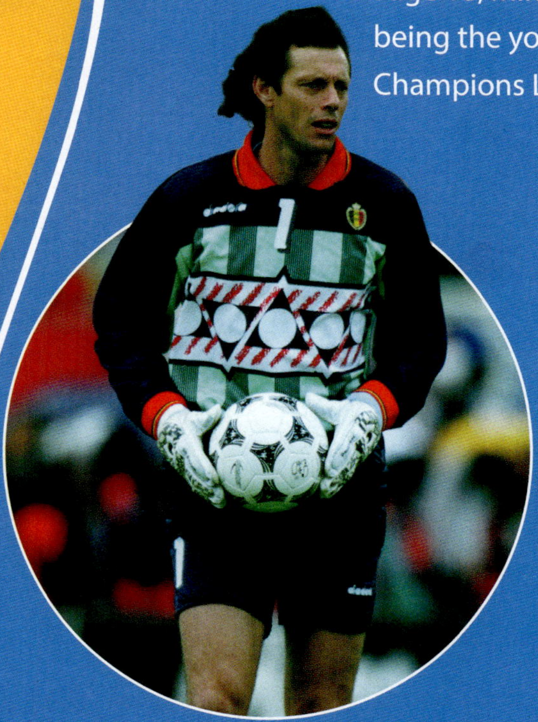

In 1994, former Benfica goalie Michel Preud'homme became the first player in history to receive an award for best goalkeeper in a World Cup.

The Coaches

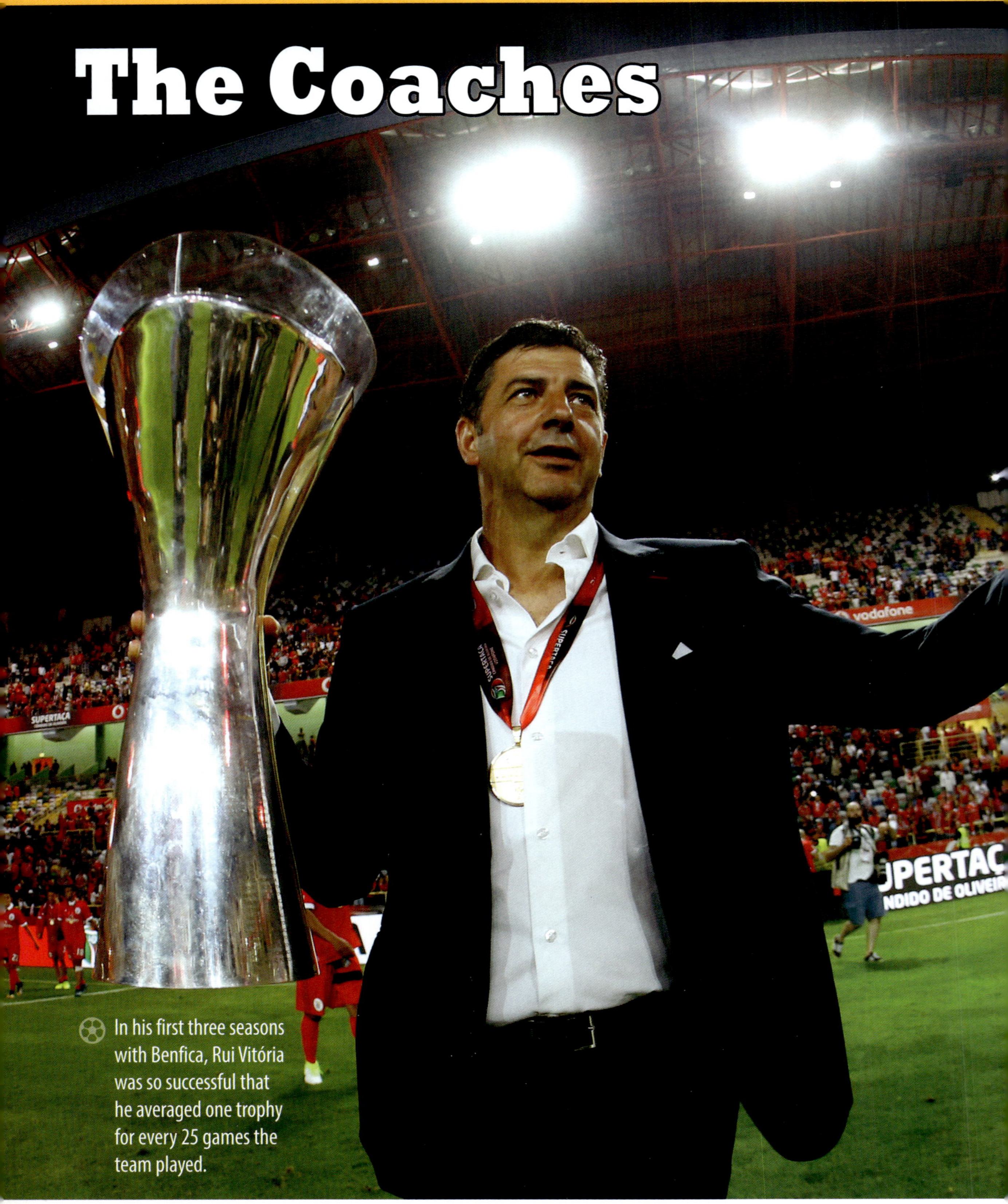

In his first three seasons with Benfica, Rui Vitória was so successful that he averaged one trophy for every 25 games the team played.

Benfica has been coached by many men. The longest-serving coach was one of the team's founding members, Cosme Damião. Damião was a player-coach from 1908 to 1916 and continued coaching until 1926. Benfica's yearly player awards are named after Damião, the "Father of Benfica." Béla Guttmann coached Benfica to its first European victory. Jorge Jesus is the club's most successful coach of all time. The team's current coach is Rui Vitória.

RUI VITÓRIA Rui Vitória was hired to lead Benfica in 2015. Vitória is calm and even-tempered on the sideline. Tactically, he is known for starting a game with intense offensive pressure on the ball in order to score. Vitória's second-half coaching focuses on defense, maintaining the score established from the first half's pressure. Benfica has won more than 70 percent of its games under his leadership.

JORGE JESUS Jorge Jesus led Benfica to 10 titles in six seasons. Jesus also took the team to its ninth and tenth European finals. Known as being very outspoken and dynamic, his coaching style centers on attacking defensively and pressuring the ball. Against these tactics, opposing teams have trouble getting past midfield and cannot score easily. Jesus coached at Benfica from 2009 to 2015.

BÉLA GUTTMANN Béla Guttmann coached about 20 different teams and rarely stayed at any for longer than two seasons. Under his leadership, Benfica won two European Championships. Guttmann's request for a pay raise after the 1962 European Championship was turned down by Benfica's owners. He stormed out, stating that Benfica would never win a European Championship again. Although the team has made a European final twice more since that day, they have never won. The club refers to this as "Guttmann's Curse."

Fans Around the World

More than 50,000 fans fill Estádio da Luz for Benfica home matches. Benfica ranks 12th for attendance among all European soccer clubs.

Benfica is a member-owned club. Members are called *sócios*, "partners," and they elect leaders and participate in general assemblies to make policies for the club. Benfica fans are known as *Benfiquistas*, "supporters of Benfica." There are fan groups around the world known as *Casas do Benfica*, or "Benfica Houses." Benfica has 14 million fans worldwide. The club has more than 1 million followers on Twitter and 3.6 million Facebook followers.

During Benfica matches, **ultras** gather to sing songs and hold up banners. At the start of every match, fans sing "Ser Benfiquista." The song is the club's official anthem and is about how Benfica rose above its humble beginnings with talent and bravery.

Fan Traditions

#1 The Lisbon Derby, a match between Benfica and Sporting, is one of Portugal's biggest domestic soccer games. It draws fans from all over the country.

#2 There is an area in the Museu Benfica Cosme Damião dedicated to the club's fans called "Journey to the Heart of Benfica." It has constantly changing images of fans on large screens.

Legends of the Past

Many great players have suited up for SL Benfica. A few of them have become icons of the team and the city it represents.

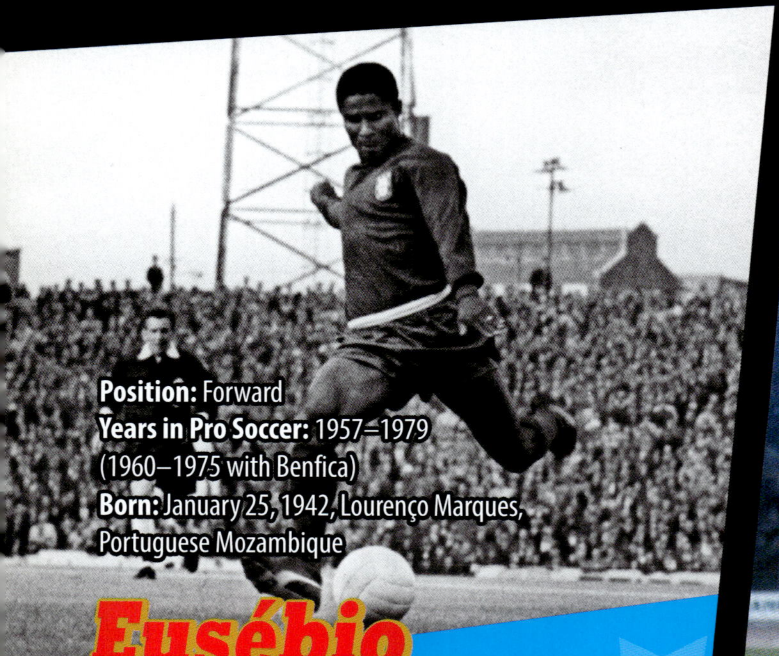

Position: Forward
Years in Pro Soccer: 1957–1979 (1960–1975 with Benfica)
Born: January 25, 1942, Lourenço Marques, Portuguese Mozambique

Eusébio

Born Eusébio da Silva Ferreira, this dynamic **striker** was one of Benfica's most memorable players. He was nicknamed "the Black Panther," "the Black Pearl," and "*o Rei*," or "the King." Eusébio was Benfica's top scorer of all time, with more than 600 goals in all matches, including **friendlies**. He was the Primeira Liga's leading scorer seven times. Eusébio led Benfica to its second European championship in 1962 and scored nine goals in the 1966 World Cup for Portugal. Eusébio is considered one of the greatest soccer players of all time, and the greatest Portuguese player ever.

Humberto Coelho

Humberto Coelho started and ended his playing career at Benfica. He was one of the team's captains and scored 77 Primeira Liga goals. Coelho is considered one of Portugal's all-time best **defenders**. Standing at just over 6 feet (183 centimeters) tall, he was quite intimidating on the field. Coelho was a natural leader who possessed great skill and a strong understanding of the game. After retiring from play, Coelho managed several teams and now serves as Vice President of the Portuguese Football Federation.

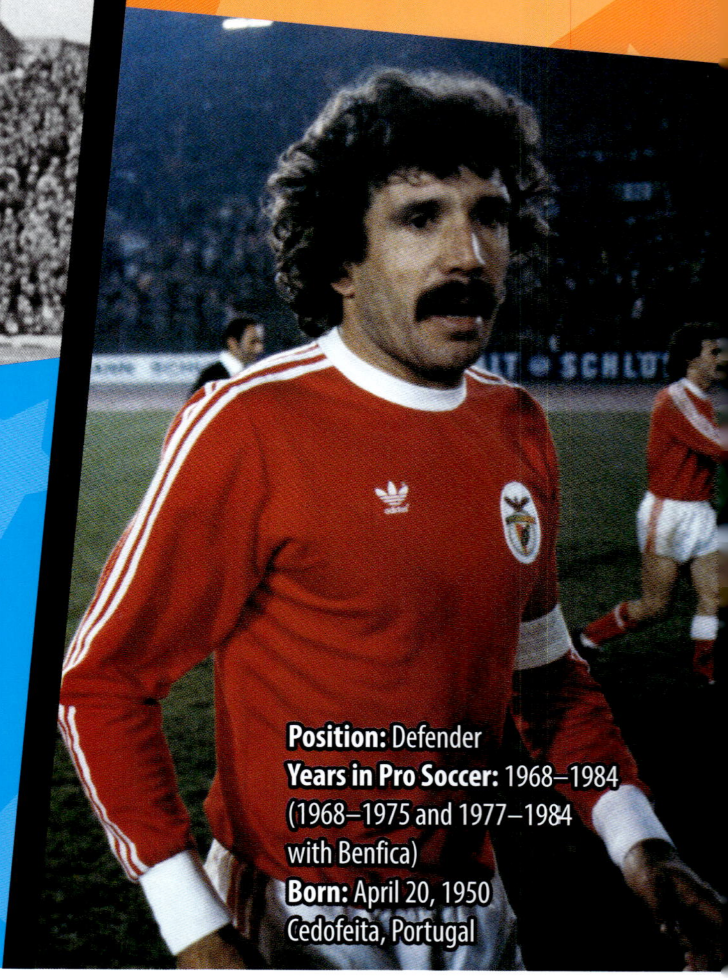

Position: Defender
Years in Pro Soccer: 1968–1984 (1968–1975 and 1977–1984 with Benfica)
Born: April 20, 1950 Cedofeita, Portugal

Luisão

Luisão was born Ânderson Luís da Silva. He played 15 seasons at Benfica. Luisão holds multiple individual records with Benfica, including most trophies won and longest-serving captain. He helped Benfica win its first league title in more than a decade in his second season. This was the first of many during his time with the team. Luisão is often praised for his passing skills, winning balls in the air, and scoring on **set pieces** such as corner kicks and free kicks. He debuted for the Brazilian National team in 2001 and played in 41 international matches. Luisão was an intimidating defender. He had a reputation for being extremely passionate and enthusiastic about the game, both on and off the field.

Position: Defender
Years in Pro Soccer: 1999–2018
(2003–2018 with Benfica)
Born: February 13, 1981, Amparo, Brazil

Mário Coluna

Midfielder Mário Coluna spent the majority of his career with Benfica. He was part of the team's back-to-back European championship-winning teams and scored in both finals. Coluna scored 150 goals in 677 total games for Benfica and served as team captain. Nicknamed "the Sacred Monster," Coluna also captained the Portuguese national team during the 1966 World Cup, during which Portugal lost to England in the semifinals. Coluna was very kind, soft-spoken, and well-respected. He was supposed to take the penalty kick in the 1962 European Cup final but allowed Eusébio to take it instead, giving the teenager his first goal in a major competition.

Position: Midfielder
Years in Pro Soccer: 1954–1972
(1954–1970 with Benfica)
Born: August 6, 1935
Inhaca, Mozambique

Stars of Today

Today's SL Benfica team is made up of many young, talented players who have proven that they are among the best in the league.

Jardel

Jardel Vieira, known simply as Jardel, played for multiple clubs in Brazil before signing with Benfica. He has played in more than 200 games for the Eagles. Jardel is the team's current captain and has led the team to 12 trophies. He is prone to fouls in defensive tackles, but is known for winning balls in the air, passing, and intercepting balls on the ground. Jardel began as a sub for starting defenders at Benfica but worked his way into a starting position. He recently became a Portuguese citizen and signed an extended contract with Benfica.

Position: Defender
Years in Pro Soccer: 2004–Present (Joined Benfica in 2011)
Born: March 29, 1986, Florianópolis, Brazil

Eduardo Salvio

Eduardo Salvio is a versatile player. He does well in both offensive and defensive positions and has played forward, midfield, and defense for Benfica. Salvio has helped Benfica win four national championships in a row since 2014. Recognized for his dribbling and goal-scoring ability, he has earned 60 goals for the club. He is also a member of the Argentine national team. Salvio played a defensive role for Argentina in two World Cup matches in 2018.

Position: Forward
Years in Pro Soccer: 2008–Present (Joined Benfica in 2010)
Born: July 13, 1990, Avellaneda, Argentina

Rafa Silva

Rafa Silva began his professional career with Liga NOS team Feirense before signing with Benfica. Silva is comfortable on both the left and right sides of the field and has scored goals from both sides. Known as a skilled dribbler, he is good at maintaining possession of the ball. Silva is a quick thinker who is capable of creating scoring opportunities for himself and his teammates. He was also a member of the Portuguese national team that won the UEFA European Championship in 2016.

Position: Midfielder/Forward
Years in Pro Soccer: 2012–Present (Joined Benfica in 2016)
Born: May 17, 1993, Vila Franca de Xira, Portugal

Pizzi

Pizzi's real name is Luís Miguel Afonso Fernandes . He wore Braga and Atlético Madrid uniforms before joining the Eagles in 2013. Pizzi's strengths include crossing, passing, and taking set pieces. He likes to play long balls and dribble downfield. Pizzi is considered a better offensive player than defensive, even though he can play both roles. He has made just under 200 appearances with Benfica and has scored almost 40 goals. Pizzi is a member of the Portuguese national team and played in one World Cup qualifying match in 2017, as well as several international friendlies.

Position: Midfielder
Years in Pro Soccer: 2007– Present
(Joined Benfica in 2013)
Born: October 6, 1989, Bragança, Portugal

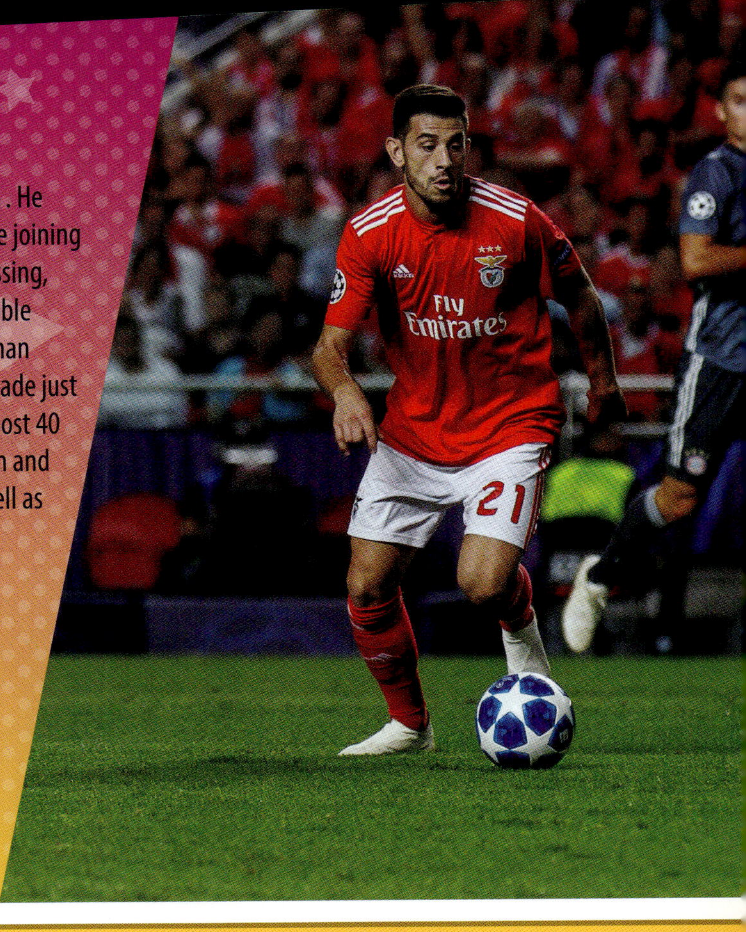

All-Time Records

19

Most Trophies

Luisão collected 19 trophies with Benfica, more than any other player in the team's history.

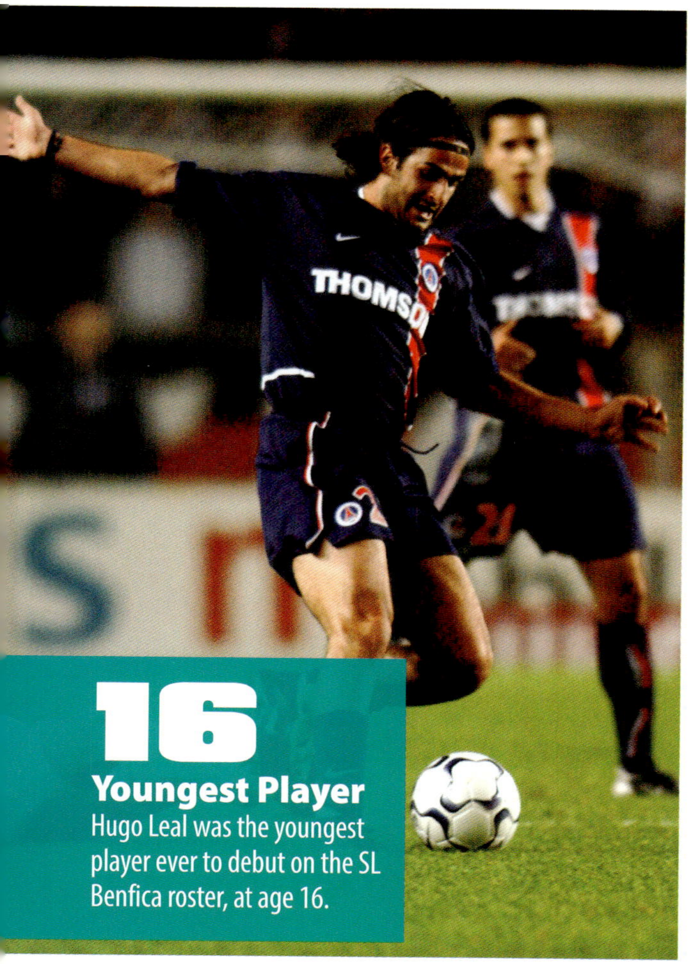

16

Youngest Player

Hugo Leal was the youngest player ever to debut on the SL Benfica roster, at age 16.

473

Most Goals Scored

Eusébio is Benfica's top goal scorer, with a total of 473 official goals.

64,591

Record Attendance

Fans broke the attendance record at Estádio da Luz in 2017 when 64,591 people gathered to watch Benfica win its fourth national championship in four years.

48

Longest Win Streak

Benfica was unbeaten for 48 games in a row from 1963 to 1965.

Timeline

Throughout the team's history, SL Benfica has had many memorable events that have become defining moments for the team and its fans.

1904
Cosme Damião and others officially establish Sport Lisboa.

In 1908, Sport Lisboa and Grupo Sport Benfica merge into one club, Sport Lisboa e Benfica.

1930
Benfica wins the Portuguese Cup for the first time.

1936
Benfica wins the Primeira Liga title for the first time and goes on to win it the following two years.

1954
Benfica begins playing in the massive Estádio da Luz.

1890 | 1900 | 1910 | 1920 | 1930 | 1940 | 1950

The Future
Benfica was in the top three of the Primeira Liga for the 2018–19 season. The team is ranked in UEFA's top 25. With consistency in coaching and a roster filled with young players, Benfica has the potential to keep dominating Portuguese soccer, and perhaps even finally break Guttmann's Curse.

2009
Jorge Jesus is appointed Benfica's head coach. He leads the team to 10 titles in six seasons.

1960 | 1970 | 1980 | 1990 | 2000 | 2010 | 2020

1961
Under Béla Guttmann, Benfica wins the first of two consecutive European Cups.

In 2003, Estádio da Luz is demolished and a new, more modern Estádio da Luz is built in its place.

2011
Benfica reaches the semifinal of the Europa League, the team's first major European competition since 1994.

2017
Benfica wins its first ever "tetra," or four league titles in a row.

Write a Biography

Life Story

A person's life story can be the subject of a book. This kind of book is called a biography. Biographies often describe the lives of people who have achieved great success. These people may be alive today, or they may have lived many years ago. Reading a biography can help you learn more about a great person.

Get the Facts

Use research in the library and on the internet to find out more about your favorite soccer player. Learn as much about him or her as you can. What position does he or she play? What are his or her statistics in important categories? Has he or she set any records? Also, be sure to write down key events in the person's life. What was this player's childhood like? What has he or she accomplished off the field? Is there anything else that makes this person special or unusual?

Use the Concept Web

A concept web is a useful research tool. Read the questions in the concept web on the following page. Answer the questions in your notebook. Your answers will help you write a biography.

Concept Web

Write a Biography

Adulthood
- Where does this individual currently reside?
- Does he or she have a family?

Your Opinion
- What did you learn from the books you read in your research?
- Would you suggest these books to others?
- Was anything missing from these books?

Childhood
- Where and when was this person born?
- Describe his or her parents, siblings, and friends.
- Did this person grow up in unusual circumstances?

Accomplishments off the Field
- What is this person's life's work?
- Has he or she received awards or recognition for accomplishments?
- How have this person's accomplishments served others?

Help and Obstacles
- Did this individual have a positive attitude?
- Did he or she receive help from others?
- Did this person have a mentor?
- Did this person face any hardships?
- If so, how were the hardships overcome?

Accomplishments on the Field
- What records does this person hold?
- What key games and plays have defined his or her career?
- What are this person's stats in categories important to his or her position?

Work and Preparation
- What was this person's education?
- What was his or her work experience?
- How does this person work?
- What is the process he or she uses?

Trivia Time

Take this quiz to test your knowledge of SL Benfica. The answers are printed upside down under each question.

1 Who is considered the "Father of Benfica"?

A. Cosme Damião

2 What are the names of the two live eagles owned by Benfica?

A. Victory and Glory

3 Who holds the record for being the youngest goalkeeper to play in the Champions League?

A. Mi e Svilar

4 Why did Béla Guttmann "curse" Benfica?

A. The club would not give him a pay raise.

5 What are *Casas do Benfica*, or "Benfica Houses"?

A. Benfica's fan groups

6 During which year did fans break the attendance record at Estádio da Luz?

A. 2017

7 How many European Championships has Benfica won?

A. Two

8 Who is Benfica's most successful coach of all time?

A. Jorge Jesus

9 What is the meaning of Benfica's motto, *E pluribus unum*?

A. "Out of many, one"

Key Words

clubs: athletic teams or organizations

decorated: awarded many trophies or titles

defenders: also called "backs," players who play in front of the goal and stop the other team from scoring

forward: a player on a soccer team who normally plays closest to the opponent's goal and tries to score goals

friendlies: matches or games that do not count toward league standings or tournament rankings for a sports team

goalkeeper: also called a "goalie," the player responsible for keeping the ball from going into the goal, and the only player who is allowed to pick up the ball

kit: standard attire and equipment worn by soccer players, including shirts, shorts, socks, and shin guards

midfielder: a soccer player who plays between the forwards and defenders and can take either a defensive or offensive role

set pieces: situations in which the ball is returned to play after a penalty or foul; some examples include corner kicks and free kicks

striker: a forward player who is the team's primary scorer

ultras: soccer fans known for extreme support of a club

Index

Coelho, Humberto 20
Coluna, Mario 21

Damião, Cosme 7, 9, 17, 19, 26, 30

Estádio da Luz 5, 8, 9, 10, 11, 18, 25, 26, 27, 30
Estádio das Amoreiras 9
Estádio do Campo Grande 9
Eusébio 9, 20, 21, 24

FC Porto 4

Guttmann, Béla 17, 27, 30

Jardel 22
Jesus, Jorge 17, 27, 30

Leal, Hugo 24
Lisbon Derby 19
Luisão 21, 24

Pizzi 23
Preud'homme, Michel 15
Primeira Liga 4, 5, 7, 11, 12, 20, 26, 27

Salvio, Eduardo 22
Silva, Rafa 23
Sporting CP 4, 7, 11
Svilar, Mile 15, 30

uniforms 12, 13, 15

Varela, Bruno 15
Vitória, Rui 5, 16, 17
Vlachodimos, Odysseas 14, 15

Log on to www.av2books.com

AV² by Weigl brings you media enhanced books that support active learning. Go to www.av2books.com, and enter the special code found on page 2 of this book. You will gain access to enriched and enhanced content that supplements and complements this book. Content includes video, audio, weblinks, quizzes, a slide show, and activities.

AV² Online Navigation

Audio
Listen to sections of the book read aloud.

Book Pages
AV² pages directly correspond to pages in the book.

Video
Watch informative video clips.

Embedded Weblinks
Gain additional information for research.

Key Words
Study vocabulary, and complete a matching word activity.

Try This!
Complete activities and hands-on experiments.

Quizzes
Test your knowledge.

Slide Show
View images and captions, and prepare a presentation.

AV² was built to bridge the gap between print and digital. We encourage you to tell us what you like and what you want to see in the future.

Sign up to be an AV² Ambassador at www.av2books.com/ambassador.

Due to the dynamic nature of the Internet, some of the URLs and activities provided as part of AV² by Weigl may have changed or ceased to exist. AV² by Weigl accepts no responsibility for any such changes. All media enhanced books are regularly monitored to update addresses and sites in a timely manner. Contact AV² by Weigl at 1-866-649-3445 or av2books@weigl.com with any questions, comments, or feedback.